The Fire That Was Meant to Touch

One Soul's Spiritual Journey Back to the One She Always Knew

The Fire That Was Meant to Touch

One Soul's Spiritual Journey Back to the One She Always Knew

Sharon Washington

"When you pass through the waters, I will be with you;
and when you pass through the rivers, they will not sweep over you.
When you walk through the fire, you will not be burned;
the flames will not set you ablaze."

Isaiah 43:2

Privacy Note:
Out of respect for the privacy of others, real names have not been used in this book. This story reflects my personal journey, and while the emotions and experiences are deeply real, I've chosen to honor the identity of those involved by keeping their names private. This is my truth, told with grace.

Published by Rose of Sharon Ministry
ISBN: 979-8-9930753-1-0

First printing, 2025

This book is dedicated to…

To the one who never knew the impact he had.
Your story awakened mine, and without knowing it, you inspired this book.
You became the spark that stirred my soul, the flame that led me back to God.

To the one who thought she was going crazy.
You're not. You're just waking up. This is for you.

To my children. May you always choose healing over holding on.
May you always choose God.

To my grandchildren. May you forever walk in love, faith, and purpose.

To the woman I buried, the woman I'm becoming, and the woman who rose.

To the reader. May these pages remind you that your pain has purpose,
your fire has meaning, and your soul is not alone.

And finally, to God, the One who never let go when I ran.
This fire was always Yours.

In Loving Memory of My Mother

Because You Believed in Me

You knew who I was before I ever did.
I'll never forget the look on your face when you handed me that Dake's Bible just weeks before you passed.
It was as if you already knew God had something special planned for my life,
and you were gently making sure I wouldn't forget who I was called to be.

The truth is, I didn't see it then. But you did.

I still wish I could sit with you and talk like we used to.
I wish I could tell you that I'm back now, walking in the purpose you always believed was mine.
I miss you so much, and even now, years later, I feel your absence like it was yesterday.
The pain of losing you is still here, but I know you are in a better place.

This book is part of your legacy.
With every page, every tear, and every word, I pray I'm honoring you.
I hope you know that your prayers continue to carry me even now, that your love still surrounds me, and that the lessons you taught me continue to guide my steps.

Your faith in me, your unwavering belief in my purpose,
and the strength you instilled in me are still my foundation every day.

Even in your absence, your spirit whispers encouragement,
your faith reminds me to keep going,
and your love reminds me to never give up.

I carry you with me in everything I do,
and I hope that through these words, a part of you lives on.

Table of Contents

Author's Note

This book was written by a woman, a real woman with a real heart, a real calling, and a real fire. These words did not come from imagination. They came from encounters, from the middle of the night, from tear-stained journals, and from the voice of God whispering, "Write it down." Every chapter was born out of surrender, and every page carries something sacred. This is my truth, my healing, and my awakening. I did not write this to impress you. I wrote it because I lived it and because I survived it.

If you find yourself wondering about the people or experiences mentioned in these pages, know this: my story is my truth. It is a journey of pain, growth, and grace. I hope it inspires, encourages, and connects with anyone who reads it.

This book is written from my personal experiences and faith journey. While it includes moments where I noticed patterns or connections, these are shared as part of my testimony and how I believe God was guiding me. It is not written to promote confusion or misunderstandings, nor to endorse practices or beliefs outside of God's Word.

This is the story of a soul finding its way back to God, the ultimate source of love and healing.

~ Sharon Washington

Preface

Some things in life don't come with explanations, only feelings. Feelings that wake you in the night. A fire in your soul you can't ignore. You don't always know where it's leading, but somehow… you know it's God.

That's how this journey began. Not with clarity, but with a calling I couldn't shake. I had built a peaceful life in another country, one where no one used the name tied to my purpose. I tried to hide and let go of ministry, titles, and dreams I didn't ask for.

But God doesn't forget what He placed in you. You can run, but eventually, the call catches up.

This book tells the story of what happens when it does. The fire didn't come to destroy me; it came to awaken me. Love showed up in unexpected form. Pain led me to meaning. And the stirring gave way to surrender.

This isn't just a story of a woman who ran. It's about a woman Heaven wouldn't stop chasing.

If you've ever questioned your sanity, wrestled with your calling, or wondered if your pain had a purpose, this is for you.

I'm no expert. I'm just someone who's been there. And I'm still standing in the fire.

Introduction

Some stories are told because they need to be. This is one of those stories. I did not write this from a perfect place; I wrote it while I was still healing. I did not have all the answers, but I had the courage to be honest.

This is not a fantasy. It is a real journey. One where I ran, prayed, questioned, fell, and got back up. Not by my strength, but because God would not let me stay stuck.

This is about fire, not the kind that destroys, but the kind that awakens and purifies. What looked like heartbreak was really God pulling me back to purpose. This is not about romance. It is about alignment, a love that leads you back to God and reminds you who you are.

You might see parts of your own story here. Maybe even pieces you forgot. If you do, I pray healing begins for you too. You are not here by accident.

This is only the small beginning of what God is doing, and I believe the same is true for you. So, take a breath, open your heart, and let us begin.

With love and purpose,
Sharon

The Dream

Chapter 1: **The Dream**

It all started with a dream. I had it sometime around October or November of 2024. In the dream, I saw a tall, slender man with brown skin. I remember exactly what he was wearing. He had a rust-colored jacket and blue jeans. He was standing in what looked like either a bus station or an airport. People were sitting and standing around, going about their day, but my eyes were drawn to him.

He leaned casually against a pole, looking out the window with a calm smile on his face, as if he was simply waiting. I do not know where I was coming from, but I was trying to get to him. In my heart, I felt love for him, and I sensed that he loved me in return. It was the kind of love that felt deep in my heart, the kind that needs no explanations because you feel completely seen and understood.

I could see myself moving toward him, but I never reached him. I woke up before I could get there. The dream felt so real that I looked around my room, almost expecting him to still be there. I kept thinking about that dream. Even after I woke up, the feeling from it did not go away. I sat there for a while, replaying the way he stood, the way the light touched his face, and the strange calm it gave me. It awakened something in me.

What I did not realize at the time was that the dream came after a quiet pattern had already begun. Back when I was living in Kuwait, I started waking up in the middle of the night at exactly 2:31 a.m. I noticed it because it happened often enough to make me wonder why. I did not attach any special meaning to the number or the time, but I remember the stillness. When I moved back to the United States, the pattern followed me.

From that point on, I went about my days with an awareness. Whether it was at church, in the grocery store, or walking down the street, I sometimes caught myself glancing around, aware of the thought that he might appear. It was not a desperate search. It was more like waiting for a letter in the mail you know will come eventually. You do not know the exact day it will arrive, but you keep checking the mailbox.

I did not know what the dream meant, but I knew it mattered. Something about it felt alive and true. My prayer life had gone quietly. I did not feel worthy enough to approach Him like I used to, yet even in that wilderness I still whispered small words to Him. That distance became a weapon against me. The enemy whispered that I did not belong in God's presence anymore. Shame can weigh you down. It does not just press on you; it tries to convince you to stay hidden.

But something began to shift after that dream. I still could not always find the words to pray, and I still felt far from God. Yet at unexpected times I would feel something stirring deep inside me. It was not sadness. It was more like a quiet ache that reminded me how much I longed for Him. Psalm 42:1 says, "As the deer pants for streams of water, so my soul pants for you, my God." That longing was steady and constant, like a gentle knock on my heart that never stopped no matter how busy life became.

God has sometimes spoken to me through dreams, and this one felt different. It felt like He was quietly preparing something good for me. In quiet moments before bed, while riding in the car, or folding laundry, I often found myself reflecting on it. It was not a needy or desperate feeling. It felt whole, safe, and familiar.

I began to believe God had a reason for showing me this man. When I woke, it felt like parting with someone I had known for a long time. The certainty I felt was unlike anything before. I was not chasing attention or validation. I longed for something genuine and shaped by God's will. That dream reminded me that such love still exists. It lit up places in my heart that had gone dark.

I was in a spiritual wilderness, but I still held on to God. I did not realize it then, but the dream was the first thread. God was already weaving together moments that would challenge me, stretch me, and slowly prepare my heart for the season ahead. Proverbs 13:12 says, "Hope deferred makes the heart sick, but a longing fulfilled is a tree of life." That dream planted hope in me. Hope may start as a quiet seed, but when you tend it, even with the smallest prayers, it will break through the soil and reach for the light.

That seed was planted deep in me, but life around me kept moving. I carried it quietly, not knowing what it would grow into, while at the same time trying to face the reality of where I was. I could sense God was preparing me for something, but I did not yet understand what. All I knew was that the next season would test the soil of my life and stretch me in ways I was not expecting.

Chapter 1 Reflection

1. When you read about the dream and its effects, what feelings did this chapter evoke in you?

____

____

____

____

2. Have you ever experienced a moment that stuck with you and seemed to have a deeper meaning, whether it was a dream or an emotion?

____

____

____

____

3. What struck you as the most poignant aspect of Sharon's experience with shame and separation from God?

____

____

____

____

4. How does the notion of love arousing something within you personally resonate with you?

____

____

____

____

5. Have you noticed any signs of recovery or rediscovery in any area of your life?

____

____

____

____

Reflection Notes

The Encounter

Chapter 2: **The Encounter**

When I moved back to America from Kuwait in June of 2024, I never imagined I would feel like a foreigner in my own country. But I did. Everything felt off. I was experiencing culture shock in a place I had once called home. Simple things like conversations, social media, and even grocery store trips suddenly felt strange, loud, and overwhelming. I longed to go back to Kuwait; the place I had made my home for six years. It was where I had grown, changed, and built a life. Nothing here felt quite right. I did not feel grounded, and honestly, I did not feel like myself. But I also knew it was time to face the truth I had been trying to bury.

Social media was never supposed to be part of my healing journey. I used it to scroll from time to time, usually looking at recipes, watching educational clips, and sometimes stumbling across a sermon or something spiritually encouraging. I was not trying to build a platform or be noticed. For me it was simply background noise in the middle of everything else, something I hardly thought about. Yet God was already planning to use it in a way I never expected.

I was scrolling and I came across a live. Something about the voice caught my attention. For some reason, I showed up more than once, even though I could not explain why. In that instance, something in me recognized the man from my dream.

When the live ended, I was overwhelmed with feelings I could not sort through. I sat in silence until the tears came. I could not tell anyone, not even my children. It felt too personal, too sacred to risk being misunderstood. So, I carried it quietly, letting it settle in my heart while I brought it before God.

In the days that followed, I tried to pray, but it was hard. Shame and guilt made me feel unworthy to go before God like I once had. Most of the time, my prayers were short and unsteady. I did not always know what to say, but I still tried, because even the smallest prayers were all I had to offer.

I wanted clarity from God. I cleared out my closet and turned that small space into a private place for prayer. I would go in, close the door, and sit in the quiet. Some days I had no words. I would cry until my tears ran out, and then I would simply rest in the stillness. My tears became my prayers. My silence became a way of surrender. Even in that quiet, I carried questions I could not put into words. I trusted that God saw the depths of my heart, even when I did not understand why I was feeling this so deeply.

Whatever this was, it would not go away. I prayed for it to fade, but instead it grew stronger. It was not a passing emotion. It was a steady awareness that pressed me to face the truth about the places in my life where I still needed God's healing.

This season felt like God was silent, pressing me to trust Him when I could not sense Him and when I could not feel Him. I thought about the people in the Bible who walked through that same silence. David wrestled with the feeling of being forgotten in Psalm 13, wondering how long God's silence would last. Job sat in ashes, wondering why God allowed so much suffering in his life. And Jesus, in His final hours, cried out on the cross, "My God, my God, why have you forsaken me?" None of these were moments of weakness. They were cries I recognized in my own spirit.

God was using this season to pull up the weeds that had been choking my spirit. I did not see it that way back then. All I knew was that my emotions were pulling at me in ways I could not always understand. But emotions were never meant to guide me. My anchor had to be His truth, His Word, even when it was hard for me to hold onto it. It was a breaking, a stripping away, and a silence I did not know how to name. It was not loud or sudden, but it was real, and I could not escape it. I did not realize it then, but the encounter was not only stirring hope, but it was also pulling on something deep inside me, like a flame I could not turn away from.

Chapter 2 Reflection

1. When you read about Sharon's unexpected encounter on social media and how profoundly it affected her spirit, what feelings did you experience?

____

____

____

____

2. Have you ever had a spiritually significant experience that you couldn't quite put your finger on but knew was greater than yourself?

____

____

____

____

3. Sharon understood that the fire she experienced was a purifying force rather than a form of punishment. In what ways has God used your own suffering or perplexity to heal you?

____

____

____

____

Reflection Notes

Drawn to the Flame

Chapter 3: **Drawn to the Flame**

As I watched the live, something shifted. It was like my soul knew that flame had been waiting, quiet, just for me. I cannot explain it fully, but it opened something. Almost like doors I thought were locked for good suddenly swung open. Some of what I felt was light, almost gentle, like God reaching toward me through it. Other times, it pressed hard. It made me look at parts of myself I had buried deep.

The stirring would not let me go. I did not know what was happening inside me, and that left me confused. I had never felt anything like this before. It was a pull, almost an ache. I carried it everywhere, and no matter what I did, I could not escape it.

I wanted to know why. Why did it go so deep? Why did it unsettle me like this? The fire pushed me to pray. Prayer became the only place I felt safe enough to break down. It was my shelter.

Even then, the ache stayed. Some days it pressed harder. Other days it sat quiet, just under the surface. But it never left. And I knew God was letting it stay. He was pulling me back, again and again.

Then the mornings came. The same way. Over and over. I would wake up at exactly 2:31 a.m. At first, I brushed it off. I told myself it was coincidence. But the more it happened, the harder it was to ignore. Not every single night, but enough. Enough to make me stop and wonder. That hour felt heavy. Like God was calling me in the silence, asking me to listen.

On some of those mornings, I stayed quiet. I opened His Word. Psalm 34:18 became the verse I clung to: "The Lord is close to the brokenhearted and saves those who are crushed in spirit." I whispered it over and over, until my breathing slowed. And then, little by little, peace would come.

This stirring in me was never about what I could see. It was not outward. It was deeper. God was showing me how even pain can draw us back to Him. Healing does not always come the way we expect. Sometimes it comes wrapped in fire. Sometimes it comes in silence. But when God is in it, even the flame that burns and exposes becomes sacred.

The flame felt like calling and refining, both at once. It stripped away comfort. It pushed me into questions. It made me search for God in ways I had not before.

I did not realize it then, but the flame was digging into places I thought were gone. Old wounds began to rise. Wounds I had only covered, never healed. It hurt. I did not know why God allowed it. But the fire demanded my attention. It pulled my prayers. It pressed me into questions I could not answer.

Looking back, I see now it was only the beginning. Being drawn to a flame was the start of something deeper, something God would use to uncover wounds I could no longer avoid.

Chapter 3 Reflection

1. What part of Sharon's experience of being drawn to the flame and stirred in prayer spoke most deeply to you?

____

____

____

____

2. Have you ever experienced a spiritual awakening triggered by someone else's story or presence?

____

____

____

____

3. What are your thoughts on the difference between obsession and yearning, and have you experienced one or both in your own life?

____

____

____

____

4. Have you ever received what felt like divine signs or synchronicities? How did they make you feel?

____

____

____

____

5. In what ways have you felt God drawing near to you during times of brokenness or struggle?

____

____

____

____

Reflection Notes

His Story Dug Up My Wounds

Chapter 4: **His Story Dug Up My Wounds**

It was too much, too soon. I did not realize it at first, but being in that space stirred something deep inside me, something I thought had been put to rest. Old anxieties, buried memories, and shadows I had worked hard to silence began to rise again. The parts of me I had locked away started speaking, and I could no longer ignore them. I had tucked that part of myself away so tightly that I stopped praying about it and even stopped thinking about it. But now, God was gently lifting the lid. He was not punishing me. He was asking me to take another look. What I thought was healed had only been hidden.

I ordered a book, not realizing God would use the author's words to uncover what I had buried. As I turned the pages, it felt like walking back through my own history with a flashlight I had never carried before. The words did not just describe hurt. They gave it weight, the kind of ache that sits in your chest until you can hardly breathe. The author's story mirrored mine so closely that I sometimes had to put the book down and gather myself.

Sometimes it is easy to know the Word without truly living it. People can quote Scripture yet not walk it out in their daily lives. I have come to see that knowing Scripture is not the same as letting it shape who we are. Transformation only happens through surrender, because without it, God cannot truly change a life. Speaking Scripture is easy. Letting it transform your heart takes surrender.

There was one sentence I read, and it stayed with me. I kept going back to it, even after I was done with the book: "The pain you feel today is the strength you will feel tomorrow." Each time I read it, it reached deeper, pulling up memories I thought were buried, questions I had avoided, and hopes I had let go of. That one line reminded me that pain can be a tool in God's hands, shaping what we cannot change on our own. Could it be that even this mirrored pain was part of His good work in me?

I cried through the pages, and when I finished, the tears kept falling. I cried because the author's story echoed mine. I cried because it was terrifying to see myself so clearly in another person's grief. But most of all, I cried because I could sense God shifting something inside me.

It was as if He brushed away dust so I could finally see where I had been and where He was leading me.

Old wounds stirred again. Memories I thought were healed rose to the surface, waiting for the right moment to be uncovered. The rawness of the author's honesty gave me permission to open my own story without shame. That openness uncovered places in me that still needed God's touch.

I started journaling daily, sometimes twice a day, pouring out prayers and thoughts I could not say out loud. Each page carried a release I could not find in spoken words. Writing became the way I let it out.

I prayed without always knowing what to pray for. I only knew something was stirring in me that was bigger than emotion. It felt sacred. Whatever this was, it was leading me closer to God, not away from Him.

The pain brought tears. It pushed me to my knees in ways I had not felt in years. Some prayers poured out in words, some in silence, and some in tears I could not hold back. I cried for my own healing. I did not know all the details, but sorrow has a sound, and I recognized it within the author's story. The book did not just remind me of my wounds. It exposed them, dragging into the light the places I had worked hard to bury.

God used the author's words I was reading to save me. I do not say that lightly. The testimony did not just inspire me. It broke something open. What God had hidden deep inside of me beneath silence and pain came pouring out because truth unlocked it.

I came to deeply respect the honesty woven through those pages. The words themselves carried a weight beyond explanation. Heaven knew it, and I felt it too. God used that truth as a spark to stir up what I had buried for so long.

That was when I realized this was not about emotion alone. God was waking something in me. Reading those words was like holding a mirror up to my face and seeing pieces of myself I thought were gone. I was not reliving the ache to stay stuck in it. I was facing it because God was showing me it still mattered. Psalm 139:23–24 became my prayer: "Search me, God, and know my heart; test me and know my anxious thoughts. See if there is any offensive way in me and lead me in the way everlasting."

The mind does not forget what we try to bury. It holds the hurt we silence, the lies we believe, and the feelings we never speak. The author's testimony became the doorway God used to break through the walls I built. Once His light entered, I could not hide anymore. This was more than memory. It was spiritual.

I had to learn to separate God's voice from my own. Sometimes what we think is God is really our past, our fears, or our wounds. The Holy Spirit brings conviction in love. His voice aligns with Scripture and always leads toward peace. My own thoughts wanted to protect me, but protection can sometimes keep you stuck.

In those moments I knew that only God's voice could settle what was rising in me. Little by little, He made it clear. God was gently tugging at my heart, reminding me of who I truly was. Not the version shaped by trauma, not the one weighed down by shame, but the one He had loved from the very beginning.

This stirring was not the end of anything. It was the start of something I could no longer ignore. It drew me toward a flame that both unsettled and steadied me, urging me to face places within myself I had long tried to outrun.

What I did not realize was that this stirring would soon collide with places in my story I had long ignored. The flame I felt inside was preparing me to face an earlier season of my life, a time when I had been running, convinced I could escape the very thing God was calling me to.

Chapter 4 Reflection

1. What emotions surfaced for you as Sharon described how old wounds were stirred by the story she read?

____

____

____

____

2. Can you recall a time when your subconscious mind reacted before your conscious thoughts could catch up? What did that reveal to you?

____

____

____

____

3. In what ways have unhealed places in your life shaped how you see yourself or your purpose today?

____

____

____

____

4. Have you ever run from your calling because of internal fears or old beliefs about yourself? What might those fears be rooted in?

____

____

____

____

5. What would it look like to let God heal the hidden parts of you that no one else sees—even the parts buried deep in your subconscious?

____

____

____

____

Reflection Notes

The Jonah Season

Chapter 5: **The Jonah Season**

It did not all happen at once, but deep down, I knew I was running. I did not want to fulfill God's request. After all the pain I had gone through, the rejection, the weariness, and the disillusionment, I no longer wanted the weight of ministry on my shoulders. I was not just tired. I was finished. So, I left.

I moved to Kuwait, as far as I could from everything familiar, hoping the distance would also create a spiritual separation. At first, I convinced myself it was just a fresh start in a new country with a slower pace and a different culture. I told myself I was there to experience life differently, to reset my priorities. But deep down, I knew this was not only about moving, but this was also my attempt at a spiritual escape.

I wanted to disappear, not completely, but enough to hide the part of me that had been crushed by ministry, the part that had been judged, misunderstood, and worn thin. In Kuwait, no one knew who I was spiritually, and I kept it that way. I never introduced myself as a preacher. I never mentioned my calling. I tucked that part of me away as if it did not exist.

I did not reject God, but I tried to quiet the part of me that had once stood boldly for Him. I began learning about Islam, curious about the culture and beliefs of the country I was living in. I even memorized prayers in Arabic. I told myself I was simply exploring, but in truth, I was trying to drown out the inner prompting that reminded me who I belonged to. Even when I went through the motions of those prayers, I could never finish without ending them in Jesus' name. I did not plan it. It just happened. It was as though God's truth could not be erased from my heart.

My last divorce had shattered me. It broke something deep inside. Years passed before I eventually started dating a man I will call David. I loved him. But as time went on, I realized I was the one constantly giving, always pouring into the relationship, while he only received. We dated for over a year, and I wanted marriage. Being an older man, you would think he would have been ready to settle down, but he was not in a place to commit.

I started talking about going overseas to teach. Deep down, I hoped he would stop me. I wanted him to ask me not to go and to say we should get married and build something here. Instead, he told me he was not going to stop me from following my dreams. Even though he meant it kindly, that was not what I wanted to hear.

So, I moved forward with the plan. It took months to get all of my paperwork together, and the whole time I was hoping he would change his mind and say something, anything. But he never did. The day I left, he was the one who drove me to the airport. I kept waiting for him to say, "Do not go." I looked back one last time, hoping for a sign, but all he did was wave goodbye. The silence of that goodbye said everything.

I cried the entire twenty-three-hour journey to Kuwait. Every layover, every flight, I cried. I had finally prayed, God, if he is not the one, remove him from my life. Looking back now, I can see that was God answering my prayer. But part of me still wishes I had prayed it much earlier. It would have saved me so much heartache.

When I first arrived in Kuwait, life hit me hard. The culture shock came like a wave I was not ready for, and I could not help but think about what I had gotten myself into. By the time school started in September, I had already decided that when December came and I flew home for Christmas, I would not be returning. That was the plan I held onto.

The woman who landed in Kuwait was no longer Sharon. She was Shay. I left everything behind. My ministry. My calling. I did not tell people who I really was. I did not want to talk about visions, dreams, or waking up in the early hours of the morning praying for things I could not explain, things that used to shake me to my core. I did not want any of it anymore. I just wanted to live. And for a while, I did.

Life in Kuwait felt almost unreal, like I had stepped into a dream. I found myself chasing adventures I never thought I would live. Dubai became a regular stop. I traveled to Egypt three times, and the first time I stood before the pyramids, I could not hold back the tears because seeing them had been my childhood dream. My journey stretched farther into India, Bahrain, Jordan, and Qatar. I floated in the Dead Sea and experienced the sacred moment of being baptized in the Jordan River, the very waters where Jesus Himself was baptized. That moment was holy, a kind of healing I did not even know I needed. Along the way, I picked up some Arabic, not fluent, but enough to get by. Those years were beautiful. They were wild. They felt like freedom.

But even in all of that, I still had not fully accepted who I was. Deep down, I knew God was not done with me. I could feel it, but I was not ready to surrender.

Years went by like that. Then, during my last year in Kuwait, something started to stir. It was November 2023, and I had to sign my intent letter stating I would return the following school year. So, I signed it. But the next month, in December, something shifted.

One night as I was meditating, I felt a burning in my spirit, almost like fire. In that moment, I sensed God speaking within me: It is time to return. The work that has begun in you cannot be completed in Kuwait. Philippians 1 verse 6 came alive to me: “He who began a good work in you will carry it on to completion until the day of Christ Jesus.” Those words rested in my spirit with such weight that I knew I had to go back to the United States.

I had until the end of December to change my mind and revoke my intent letter. And even after hearing from God, I still hesitated. I told myself I was going to stay in Kuwait. But every time I thought about staying, I felt that same burning deep in my stomach. I could not shake it.

Living in the Middle East did more than expose me to Islam. It also opened my eyes to Christianity in a way I had never seen before. Even though I was running, I could not ignore what God was showing me. For the first time, I began to recognize that so much of what I had once accepted in church did not fully line up with the Word of God. Scriptures were taken out of context, twisted in ways that left people feeling bound instead of free. And it was not just the preaching. Too often, church felt more like cliques than the body of Christ. If you were not in the right circle, or if you did not have something people wanted such as your time, your money, your talent, or even just their approval, you could easily feel left out.

As I wrestled with all these realizations, I began to see that part of what kept me running was not just disobedience but the fixed mindset I had carried for years. I had been shaped by traditions, opinions, and expectations about what faith and obedience were supposed to look like. Those old patterns made me believe I knew better than God, or at least that I could choose the terms of my obedience. Jonah carried a fixed mindset too. He believed Nineveh did not deserve mercy, and it caused him to run in the opposite direction of God's command. In my own way, I was doing the same. I was holding on to ways of thinking that made surrender harder than it had to be.

I did not fully process it then, because I was still trying to hide from God, but my mind was opening. Kuwait showed me that the way church was being practiced was not always the way Christ designed it. It planted something in me that I carried when I eventually came back to the United States, a resolve that I could no longer just go along to get along. Even in the middle of all these realizations, His presence would not let me go.

What I did not realize at the time was how much my running would cost me. My children are my life, and that is why it grieves me even more that I was not there for certain moments. Distance does not just separate you from a place. It makes you miss pieces of life you cannot get back. While I was hiding, life kept moving without me, and that left its own ache.

Psalm 139 verses 7 and 8 became real to me: "Where can I go from your Spirit? Where can I flee from your presence? If I go up to the heavens, you are there. If I make my bed in the depths, you are there." No matter where I went, His presence stayed with me. Even in a land far from home, even in a culture that did not share my faith, He was still there, quietly reminding me that I was His.

Over time, conviction began to grow inside me. It was steady and unshakable, a quiet awareness I could not ignore. There was no storm outside my window, but one was raging in my spirit. The more I tried to settle into life in Kuwait, the more unsettled I became. The beauty of the country and the calm of my routine could not quiet the restlessness in my soul. It was the kind of exhaustion that comes from living out of alignment with your purpose.

From that day until I left in June 2024, the burning would come and go like waves. It was not constant, but it was persistent, like a divine tugging at my spirit, a reminder that my steps were being ordered by the Lord. Some days it felt so strong I could hardly focus, as if God Himself were pulling me back into His will.

I did not know then that the next step in my journey would not just be about facing my disobedience. Something in me would have to break before I could truly turn back. But in that moment, I was still Jonah, still hiding, still avoiding the voice that would not let me go. I remained swallowed, caught in a place I did not understand, yet held by a God who refused to release me.

Chapter 5 Reflection

1. Have you ever run from something you felt God was calling you to do? What did that feel like?

____

____

____

____

2. Sharon kept her identity as a minister hidden during her time in Kuwait. Have you ever hidden a part of yourself in order to cope or feel safe?

____

____

____

____

3. What "Tarshish" have you run to in your own life?

____

____

____

____

4. Jonah's storm came on the sea, but Sharon's storm came inside her. What kind of internal storm has God used to get your attention?

____

____

____

____

5. "Running doesn't always look like rebellion." How does this statement challenge your understanding of disobedience?

____

____

____

____

Reflection Notes

Sacred Release

Chapter 6: **Sacred Release**

When I realized the thought of someone was beginning to take up space that belonged to God, I knew it was time to release it. It was not just about longing or wondering what might have been. It was about how much those thoughts were occupying my heart, how easily my mind returned to them, and how subtly my focus began to shift away from the One who mattered most. I did not want to lose what I had fought so hard to return to. I had come too far to let anything, even something I deeply valued, stand between me and the voice of God.

That is when I made the decision to release the situation. Not because it did not matter, but because it was beginning to weigh more than it was meant to. I had to turn my eyes forward and focus again on what God had called me to do. The release felt like both freedom and loss. It hurt, yet it was holy. It was not only about walking away from a person or a dream. It was about choosing God's will over my own, even when my heart did not fully understand. Obedience does not always feel like celebration. Sometimes it feels like grief. But even that grief can be sacred, a sign that you have surrendered something you deeply wanted because you want God more.

The grief was heavy and complete. It was not anger or relief. It was a quiet, aching sadness that lingered. The desire did not vanish the moment I let go. The thoughts still surfaced. The dream from Chapter 1 still lingered in my heart. What made it harder was that the attachment had felt significant. It had shaped the way I thought about love. That made the grief deeper. I was not only grieving the idea, but I was also grieving the hope, the possibility, and the value I had placed on what it represented. Still, I knew I had to surrender it, not because it was meaningless, but because it was beginning to compete with what was most important: my relationship with God.

Right in the middle of the release, God's guidance became clear to me again. Through prayer and Scripture, He reminded me of who I was, the calling on my life, and the woman He created me to be. I could not return to the distracted, emotionally fogged version of myself. I had come too far to lose clarity now. I resolved that even if the ache never left, I could not lose God. I was willing to walk away from anything if it meant walking in clarity.

That shift in perspective changed everything. For years, I thought the ache would disappear when love arrived. Now, all I wanted was God's presence. And in that presence, I found something far deeper than comfort. I found fulfillment. In this season, obedience meant more than laying down a person. It meant releasing old wounds, unhealthy ties, and emotional attachments that had no place in my life anymore. I deleted numbers, blocked contacts, removed photos and gifts, and stepped away from social media. It was not out of anger. It was because I needed room to heal.

This was more than decluttering. It was a spiritual cleanse. I was removing anything that could pull me back from where God was leading me. As I let go, my focus shifted toward Him in a deeper way. My prayer life changed. One morning, I felt a clear prompt in my heart to stop talking. So, I did. I sat on the floor of my prayer closet and simply rested in surrender. No pleading, no long lists, just stillness. Sometimes I stayed there for over an hour, quietly reflecting on Psalm 46:10, "Be still and know that I am God." I let that truth settle in deeper each time I repeated it in my heart. I could hear the faint hum of the air conditioner, the quiet ticking of a clock, and in between, the stillness seemed to wrap around me like a blanket.

There was healing in the stillness and peace in the quiet. Peace did not come instantly. Some days I felt strong. Other days I cried without having the words to explain why. But I kept showing up for my healing. Paul wrote in 1 Corinthians 15:31, "I die daily." That is what this season felt like. Each day, I surrendered the ache, the memories, the hopes, and even the dream.

Over time, peace began to settle in my heart. My worship became more intentional, my spirit more guarded. I was not just singing songs. I was protecting my walk with God. If I could speak to the version of myself still caught in longing, I would remind her that she was not forgotten, that God had not overlooked her. Her prayers were heard, and her tears were seen. Trust was still required. She was closer than she thought. And in time, the breakthrough came.

But the release was not the end. It was the doorway into a deeper journey. Letting go created the space for something new to begin, the slow work of healing within. What I laid down in this season prepared me for the inner work that was waiting. And that is where my story leads next.

Chapter 6 Reflection

1. What part of Sharon's sacred release process mirrored something you've had to surrender in your own life?

____

____

____

____

2. How do you relate to her longing for clarity and her journey from confusion to purpose?

____

____

____

____

3. What thoughts, people, or desires have you had to lay down in order to stay in alignment with God's will?

____

____

____

____

4. When have you experienced God's peace through stillness or silence? What did that moment teach you about surrender or obedience?

____

____

____

____

5. In what ways has your pain birthed purpose, and how are you being called to help others heal through your story?

____

____

____

____

Reflection Notes

The Inner Work

Chapter 7: **The Inner Work**

For a long time, I carried lies about myself and treated them like truth. I really thought I wasn't enough. I believed I had to chase love, prove myself, earn my spot, and hold on tight to people so they wouldn't leave. Deep down I tied my value to whether or not I was chosen. I told myself my voice only mattered if other people heard it and approved. So, I shrank. I adjusted. I worked myself past the limit just to feel like I belonged. But in the middle of all that, healing started whispering something different. God was telling me another story.

Those lies even shaped the way I prayed. I came to God like I had to beg Him to notice me, not realizing His eyes had been on me the whole time. Then I read Jeremiah 31:3: "I have loved you with an everlasting love; I have drawn you with unfailing kindness." His love wasn't something to earn. It was already mine. And as that truth settled in, the chains I had been dragging around started to feel lighter.

When His Spirit began pulling me in, it wasn't loud. It wasn't dramatic. It was quiet. Steady. But I couldn't ignore it. He started stirring things I didn't want to face, old wounds I had hidden behind church words and a confident smile. On the outside, it looked like I was fine. But inside, those places had never been surrendered. God's light has a way of finding the spots we try hardest to keep hidden. I ask God daily to search me and to know my heart, to test me and to know my hidden thoughts.

Resting in His presence was brand new for me. I always thought faith meant serving, working, and doing more. Sitting still felt wrong, almost uncomfortable. But then I read about how the Lord is good to those who place their hope in Him, and how waiting quietly for His salvation is a good thing. Waiting quietly wasn't laziness. It was trust. In those still moments, I started to realize God was working in ways I couldn't and in places I couldn't reach. My part was to make room for Him. To slow down enough for His peace to settle in the places fear used to live. Some days that meant nothing more than opening my Bible and sitting with one verse until it finally sank in.

That season wasn't about chasing a dream. It was about God calling me to honesty, to healing, and to intimacy with Him. I began to see how often I had covered pain with performance, tried to control things instead of trusting Him, or used spiritual words instead of real surrender. As those layers fell off, I began to understand that the Lord draws near to the brokenhearted and rescues those whose spirits feel crushed. His closeness wasn't temporary. It was steady, holding me like an anchor when everything else felt shaky. His peace pressed in against the weight I had carried, and I saw how He can bring beauty out of ashes, joy in place of mourning, and praise instead of despair.

As I released my own expectations, I started to see the woman God had actually created me to be. I didn't need anyone else to complete me or validate me. All I wanted was to be seen by Him and to live in a way that pleased Him. Journaling, which began as a place to pour out emotions, became a record of His hand on my life. Looking back through those pages, I could see His faithfulness even in the seasons when I felt completely lost. Writing reminded me to focus on what He was doing in me, not just on what I thought needed fixing around me.

For me, surrendering outcomes wasn't a lack of care. It was freedom from measuring my worth by results. I began to see that there is a season for everything, and this was my season to trust His timing instead of forcing mine. Waiting wasn't wasted time. It was shaping me. In that waiting, I discovered peace I had never known. I wasn't bracing for the next disappointment anymore. I was starting to expect His goodness, even when it showed up in ways I didn't see coming.

I began to see that God really does work all things together for the good of those who love Him. My worth was never tied to a title, a relationship, or anyone's approval. It had always been rooted in Christ. I also came to understand that God has given His children strength, love, and self-control instead of fear. That truth gave me the courage to live as though I was already enough, because in Him, I am. This wasn't just healing. It was becoming whole. It was making peace with my past, standing firm in my present, and stepping into the future with clear eyes. What God did in me was bigger than anything I thought I had lost. I don't walk like someone waiting to be chosen anymore. I walk knowing I already am.

Even so, part of me still felt stuck in the pain I had lived through. It was like the broken pieces of my story stretched all the way back to the beginning. To really understand where I was standing, I had to look back at where I came from. The roots of my choices, my strength, and even my scars ran deep into my earliest years. And before I could step into full healing, I had no choice but to go back to where it all began.

Chapter 7 Reflection

1. How have you experienced the 'lie of limitation' in your own life, and what truth is God revealing to you instead?

____

____

____

____

2. What does self-union mean to you, and how have you seen glimpses of becoming the person God created you to be?

____

____

____

____

3. Have you ever had to release something or someone you loved deeply in order to return to yourself and to God?

____

____

____

____

4. In what ways has God helped you detach from unhealthy expectations and walk in peace and purpose?

____

____

____

____

5. How does Sharon's realization about her identity in Christ shift your own perspective about healing, love, and worthiness?

____

____

____

____

Reflection Notes

Your Pain Has Purpose

Chapter 8: **Your Pain Has Purpose**

The Weight of My Childhood

Growing up, I often felt out of place, even within my own family. I was the black sheep, and I struggled to find my identity. It was not that I did not fit in; something about me felt different. On the outside, I seemed like a regular kid, but deep down, I carried hidden pain.

We did not have cell phones back then, so my days were spent either outside or playing with the Barbie dolls my mom gave me for Christmas and birthdays. What most people did not see was the weight I carried inside. There were times when I longed for a safe place where I could breathe, but it never seemed to exist.

I was teased a lot and bullied. Some kids called me "zebra" because my mother looked white, and my father was Black. Their words made me feel like I did not belong anywhere, as if who I was never enough. Even though it did not happen every day, those moments stayed with me and shaped how I saw myself for a long time. There were days I did not want to wear the new clothes my mom had bought me because I worried about what others might say. Fitting in felt impossible no matter what I did. Even when I tried to stay quiet and out of the way, I still got noticed. Teachers often called on me in class, which led some kids to call me the teacher's pet.

Some of the teasing went deeper than clothes or schoolwork. Because of my mother's complexion, I sometimes felt ashamed of who I was. When we went places as a family, I can remember ducking down in the car, hoping no one would see me with them. At that age, I only knew the embarrassment I carried. I eventually grew out of that shame, but the memory stayed.

Home did not always feel safe either. I witnessed the weight of my father's anger toward my mother, and those moments left a deep mark on me. I never knew what I might walk into after school, whether the house would be calm or shaken by fights that left me afraid to speak. My mother was the kindest woman you could ever meet, but my father struggled with alcohol, and his temper could be unpredictable. Holidays, especially Christmas, were the hardest. Sometimes his anger would spill over onto the very things my mom had worked so hard to give us.

I want to be clear. I do not share this with my embarrassing father. He is a changed man today. My story is my truth, and these are my honest feelings and experiences as a child.

I carried two heavy burdens. One was the fear of what might be happening at home. The other was the weight of being teased and bullied at school. I never told anyone about it because I did not want to be seen as weak, but the truth is, it took a toll on me in ways I could not fully explain at the time. There was no place where I truly felt safe, no place where I could just breathe.

Still, I sometimes found a small escape in the things I loved, little moments where the heaviness felt lighter, even if only for a while.

Early Attacks on My Life

Even as a young girl, I often felt different, though I couldn't explain why at the time. I sensed things that didn't make sense to me, but I didn't have the words to describe what they meant. When I was about eleven years old, I remember sitting quietly in my grandmother's kitchen when I suddenly heard a voice telling me to curse God and die. I looked around the empty room, unsure why I was hearing something when no one else was there. At that age, I didn't understand what had happened, but now I recognize it for what it truly was: the enemy trying to attack my faith before it had even formed. It was the same tactic he used in the book of Job, when Job's wife told him, "Do you still retain your integrity? Curse God and die" (Job 2:9).

Not long after, another attack came, this time against my body. My mother had baked a German chocolate cake, and for some reason, I decided to sprinkle sunflower seeds on top. After eating it, I became very ill. I was rushed to the hospital and ended up staying there for nearly a week. My fever spiked to 107 degrees, and my mother later told me that I had become almost completely unresponsive. The doctors said there was nothing more they could do. In that moment of desperation, one doctor explained to her that he was going to step outside of hospital regulations and try something different. He covered my body with bags of ice, and by God's mercy, the fever finally broke and I began to recover.

Through it all, God's hand was covering me. His protection was already preserving me for the purpose He had placed on my life.

From the Court to College

I started playing basketball at a young age and practiced every day. I would practice with my tall, athletic uncles when they played, and those moments helped me grow stronger. The more I practiced, the better I became. I played through elementary, high school, and into college. By the time I graduated high school, the work I had put in earned me a basketball scholarship. That scholarship meant my mother never had to pay for college, which was a huge relief for us during that time.

By my late teens, basketball was still a huge part of my life. Scoring in games and building confidence every time I stepped on the court gave me joy, and I thought it would always be part of my future.

During those years, I was in a relationship with my high school boyfriend, whom I will call Larry. We had started talking when I was in seventh grade. Our families were close, so it felt natural for us to be together. We had our ups and downs like most young couples, but he was the first boy I ever loved. I truly believed we would last.

That all changed during my first year of college. I became pregnant with my daughter, and I remember my basketball coach pulling me aside. He did not say the words directly, but he implied that there were "things" I could do so I could keep playing. I knew exactly what he meant. It was either choosing abortion or stopping basketball altogether. Abortion was never an option for me, so my basketball career ended that day.

Eventually, my boyfriend and I broke up. For a few years afterward, I regretted how things ended because he was my first love. Time has a way of bringing perspective, though, and I came to see things differently.

What I thought was the end of a dream was really God reshaping my life. I believed I was losing everything, but I was gaining the one thing I could never live without: my daughter. She became my greatest blessing, a living reminder that God's plans are higher than mine. I thought basketball would be my future, but God showed me that His vision was far greater, beginning with the gift of my child.

My First Marriage and the Battle for Survival

I eventually got a job at a chemical plant as a contractor, and that's where I met my first husband. At first, things were good. I really believed we could build a life together. But over time, it became clear he was dealing with struggles of his own, and those struggles spilled over onto me. I started seeing the same patterns I had lived with as a child.

There were nights I felt completely hopeless. I would drive around, dark thoughts running through my mind, wishing I could escape all the pain I was carrying. Those thoughts came more times than I can count. Eventually, I reached a breaking point and decided to leave. My daughter and I went to a shelter for battered women.

Before leaving, I felt a swirl of emotions. I was indecisive. I felt relieved, but also sad. I kept questioning whether I was making the right choice and wondering what life would look like outside of that situation.

When we got to the shelter, I honestly can't remember who brought us there. Someone from the shelter met us at a private location and guided us inside. I was overwhelmed at first. There were so many women who had been through similar things. I had to share a room, and at times I didn't feel comfortable. But at the same time, I was glad to be there. I knew we were safe.

One of the women there practiced witchcraft, which reminded me to keep praying and stay close to God. Another woman had gone through similar hardships, and we reconnected on Facebook later. My daughter was scared and trying to understand why we were there. I just had to trust God every step of the way. The shelter offered therapy, and that time became an unexpected season of healing for us.

After a while, he seemed to get himself together, and I went back to him, believing God had changed him. For a time, I felt hopeful again. I became pregnant with my son. Labor came fast, and I had planned on getting an epidural, but it didn't help. The pain was intense, and my mouth began to twist. My mother was there, and I thank God, I made it through. My son was beautiful, one of the cutest babies I had ever seen.

Later, I became pregnant with my youngest daughter. That pregnancy had complications, and the doctor said I would need a C-section. During the delivery, I drifted in and out of the sedation, but I will never forget the moment they brought her out. The doctor didn't say a word and rushed her to the NICU. I couldn't move, but I knew something was wrong. Later, they told me she had almost died and needed to stay in the NICU for a while. They said I could be discharged before her, but I refused to leave without my baby.

Even though I was in pain, stitched up, and sore, I pushed myself every day to walk to the NICU. It was slow, but I made it. I stood by her side and prayed over her, even when it took everything in me to stand. After three days, she came home. The doctors were shocked, but I wasn't. I knew it was God. The enemy had tried to take her out early, but God had a plan.

Even after the births of my children, things at home didn't change. Eventually, I knew I had to leave for good.

Held by God Through Loss

A year or two later, he ended up getting into legal trouble and was sent to prison. When he got out, he would write the kids and send them gifts. For a while, he seemed to be doing well. But I will never forget the day I was standing at the bus stop with my kids when my sister called me. She told me he had taken his life. I just stood there, numb. My heart broke not only for myself but for my children. I was angry that he left them with that image in their minds, angry that he did not think about how that moment would stay with them for the rest of their lives. They did not deserve that. But even through all of it, God kept us. He carried us through one of the hardest seasons of our lives.

My Second Marriage and the Loss of My Mother

Years later, before I started working at the bank, I met my second husband while working at a small store. He was an ordained elder, active in ministry, and I truly believed that God had brought us together. At that time, I had not yet confessed my own calling, so it felt like divine alignment. We dated, got married, and within six months I started receiving phone calls from women claiming they had been with him. They described the inside of his car in detail, and although I did not want to believe it, their words planted seeds of doubt.

I believed our marriage was part of God's timing, even though that relationship later turned painful. I am thankful I had him in my life during that season because shortly after we got married, my mother passed away. If I am honest, I do not know if I would have made it through that kind of grief without someone by my side. As much as the marriage eventually brought its own heartache, I believe God placed him there for a reason. He knew I would soon lose my mother.

Not long before she passed, my mother gave me a Dake's Bible. I do not know why she chose to give it to me then, but it felt significant. It was almost as if she knew there was something about my life that would require the Word to carry me. That Bible became a reminder that even in her last days, she was guiding me toward God and the path He had for me.

I will never forget the events around her death. One morning, God woke me up out of my sleep, and I felt something was not right. A heavy feeling came over me, a feeling I now know was the spirit of death. I did not know who it was for, but I got up and started praying. I cried out, asking God to have mercy. I remember saying, Lord, please give them another chance. Please do not let them die. I did not realize it at the time, but I was standing in the gap for my mother.

About a week later, my dad came over and told me she could not breathe. I rushed over, and when I saw her sitting on the couch, she was gasping for air and fighting to breathe. Her chest rose and fell so quickly that I knew something was terribly wrong. She could not speak. I knelt beside her and asked, Mom, are you praying? She nodded her head. She could not say anything, but she was still praying. My dad called 911, and they rushed her to the hospital.

We had only been there a few minutes when the doctor came out. He did not say much. He simply delivered the news that she was gone.

That image of her on the couch never left me. It is one of those memories that stays tucked in the corners of your mind, no matter how much time passes. Even now, I still see it sometimes. It hurt me deeply, and for a long time, I could not talk about it. It broke me in a way I cannot fully describe, and for years I did not even have the words. Over time, God has gently healed me, but that memory remains with me.

After my mother passed away, I sank into a deep depression. I did not want to do anything. I did not want to talk to anybody. I did not want to come out of my room. I just stayed in bed, crying constantly. Losing her was the worst pain I had ever felt. She was not just my mother; she was my best friend. The image of how she died that night would not leave me. I kept replaying it in my mind, her gasping for air and fighting to breathe. I could not unsee it. I felt like I had no will to go on.

One day, while I was lying in that bed, my youngest daughter, who was only about five years old at the time, walked into the room. Even at that young age, she carried a strong gift of prayer. She did not say much. She just laid her little hands on me and began to pray. When she did, I felt something shift. I felt a surge go through my body, like life itself was being breathed back into me. After that, I got up. I did not have it all together, but I started trying. I started trying to heal, facing the pain one step at a time.

From Grief to Calling

After my mother passed away, God began to deal with me about preaching His Word. At first, I did not want to believe it. I kept thinking there was no way God was calling me to preach. But the signs were undeniable. Everywhere I went, especially when we visited other churches, people would call me out prophetically and say preacher, even though I had not shared with anyone what I was feeling. It was as though God was using others to confirm what He had already placed in my heart.

I eventually started attending a church where the pastor was deeply anointed and had a powerful gift of discernment. Every time he called me up to pray, he would call me preacher. Still, I had not spoken a word about my calling. He saw it in me before I could even say it.

The burning in my spirit kept growing stronger, and I could no longer ignore it. I finally accepted what God had been showing me, and I confessed my call to the ministry.

Not long after, my pastor told me it was time for me to preach my first sermon. He gave me the date and everything. I began praying, asking God to show me what He wanted me to say. One day, while sitting on the couch reflecting on it all, a car commercial came on. They were trying to get people to buy a car, and the words flashed across the screen: Time is running out. Right then, God spoke to my spirit, and I knew. It was as if He was saying, this is the message I want you to deliver.

That became the title of my very first sermon: Wake Up: Time Is Running Out. That moment marked the beginning of my walk in what God had truly called me to do.

My Second Marriage and the Hidden Betrayal

I continued to have dreams that my second husband was being unfaithful. At first, I did not want to believe it, but the dreams became clearer and stronger, showing me things I did not want to see. Around that time, we had started going to a different church. Things were going really well for a season. We were both serving in ministry, and I eventually got ordained as an elder. We were over the evangelistic team, and it truly felt like we were walking in purpose.

Just when it seemed like everything had settled, the dreams started again. This time, I could not shake them.

Eventually, the truth came out: he was involved with someone he worked with. My heart sank. I did not want our marriage to fall apart, so I did what I knew to do. I prayed and fasted. For a while, it seemed like things got better. He came back around, and I thought we had made it through that storm.

A year or two later, the dreams returned, and I knew in my spirit something was off. He would leave the house at five in the morning and not return until late at night. The phone records confirmed what I had already seen in my dreams. Later, I found out the woman he was seeing was someone I had grown up with. That discovery shattered me.

At that point, I could not take it anymore. I filed for divorce. I tried my best to keep myself together. I still went to church, still smiled like nothing had happened, and never missed a beat. But the truth was, every time I sat on a pew, I felt like I was crumbling inside. I lifted my hands in worship, but tears streamed in private places no one could see. I greeted people with "I am blessed," even while my heart felt like it was breaking in two. Outwardly, I showed strength, but behind that mask was a woman who was falling apart.

My second divorce was the breaking point. It knocked me into a spiritual coma. Instead of drawing closer to the only One who could heal me, I found myself slowly drifting away from Him. I was still showing up physically, but spiritually, I was shutting down.

The burden grew heavier when the story was twisted, leaving me carrying what was never mine to carry. For a while, I even wondered if I was the problem. But deep down, I knew the truth. And even when I doubted myself, God still knew the truth. I continued to have dreams that my second husband was being unfaithful. At first, I did not want to believe it, but the dreams became clearer and stronger, showing me things I did not want to see. Around that time, we had started going to a different church. For a season, things seemed to be going really well. We were both serving in ministry, and I eventually got ordained as an elder. We were over the evangelistic team, and it truly felt like we were walking in purpose.

Just when it seemed like everything had settled, the dreams started again. This time, I could not shake them. Eventually, the truth came out: he was involved with someone he worked with. My heart sank. I did not want our marriage to fall apart, so I did what I knew to do. I prayed and fasted. For a while, it seemed like things got better. He came back around, and I thought we had made it through that storm.

Provision in the Wilderness

I got a job at the bank, but my heart still longed to teach. Eventually, I stepped out on faith. I put in my notice and went back to school. To help make ends meet, I worked part-time at Chick-fil-A. That was when the real struggle began.

My children's friends thought they had a lot of money because they never looked like they were struggling. I made sure of that, even if it meant I went without. Quietly, I was visiting food pantries just to keep food on the table. My children's clothes were neat, their shoes in good condition, and they always looked presentable. I sacrificed what I had to make sure they never looked like what we were going through. I never let them see me cry because I refused to let them see the weight of what I was carrying.

One afternoon, after walking through the mall, I stepped into the parking lot and unlocked my car. That was when I noticed something flying in the air. At first, I thought it was just a piece of paper, but when it landed at my feet, I saw it was a twenty-dollar bill. I picked it up, sat in my car, and then looked up and saw more bills falling all around me. The parking lot was still. No cars were moving. No people were in sight. It was as if time itself had paused.

I called my children right away. My daughter arrived quickly, and together we walked the entire lot, gathering twenty-dollar bills. By the time we finished, I had nearly one thousand dollars. That same day I paid the light bill and bought groceries. It was manna from heaven; sent at the exact moment we needed it most.

That was not the only time God provided in miraculous ways. Again and again, He blessed me financially in ways that I could not have expected. Sometimes it came through people I barely knew pressing money into my hand, and other times it came in quiet, personal ways that reminded me He had not forgotten me.

The struggle was real, but we never went without food. We never lost our home. Our needs were always met. Even after the money fell from the sky, God did not stop providing. He kept surprising me in ways I could never have imagined. Random people would walk up to me, sometimes at the store, sometimes in a parking lot, and bless me with money. I always accepted the money, but each time I did, I felt embarrassed, as if I was failing somehow. How could I take money from a stranger? How could I accept help when I had always prided myself on being independent?

But the provision kept coming. People at church, people I barely knew, would press cash into my hands after service, saying that God had told them to give it. Each time, I felt a pang of shame, like I was failing somehow. I had to swallow my pride and let them bless me, even as my inner voice screamed that I should be the one helping, not the one receiving.

There were times when I would go home feeling undeserving. Yet, even then, God kept reminding me that I was not forgotten. He was teaching me humility and stripping away my pride and self-sufficiency.

I was humbled by the many ways God provided. At first, I resented the feeling of dependence and the need to go to food shelters, the need to accept what was given to me.

I had tried so hard to maintain a façade of strength, of control. I did not want anyone to see the weight I was carrying. But slowly, I came to understand that God had not forgotten me. He was using these moments to teach me a lesson in humility.

Each dollar, each meal, each unexpected provision was a reminder of His love and faithfulness. It was not about the money itself but about the way God cared for me in my brokenness. He met me in the wilderness, and He did not leave me there.

Those were hard years, but they are behind me now. They remind me of how God took care of me, but they no longer define who I am. Back then, He was beginning the work of transformation, teaching me lessons I could not see at the time. That season was years ago, yet it became the foundation of the woman I have since grown into.

Chapter 8 Reflection

1. Looking back over your life, can you see how some of your deepest pain became the doorway to your purpose?

____

____

____

____

2. What personal patterns have you had to break in order to start healing and moving forward?

____

____

____

____

3. Have you ever questioned your worth because of someone else's actions or abandonment? How did God remind you of your value?

____

____

____

____

4. What has been one of your "fire" moments, the kind that hurt but also refined you? What did it burn away?

____

____

____

____

5. How have your spiritual gifts or dreams led you closer to your calling, even when you did not want them at first?

____

____

____

____

Reflection Notes

Becoming Her

Chapter 9: **Becoming Her**

What I received in that season was not what I had imagined, but it was far greater. It was something I never even knew to ask for. What I thought I would find in another person, God revealed in Himself. In that discovery, I uncovered a deeper kind of wholeness, a union with the God who had always been right beside me and with the woman I had buried under layers of shame, fear, disappointment, and longing.

For years, I looked outside myself for validation. I kept waiting for someone else to affirm my worth, to prove I mattered. But this season was different. This time it was about coming home to the version of me that had been waiting all along. She had been there, quiet but present, waiting for me to finally see her. I began to realize something: God had been my steady source long before I recognized it. He had been the one holding me together, even though I was busy handing my identity away to others who could never carry it.

That season was not about pursuit. It was about surrender. Renewal came but so did breaking. The hard shell I had been living in finally cracked. I realized walking with God is not usually one loud, dramatic moment. Most of the time, it is found in small steps of obedience, taken day by day. Each one reshaped me and drew me closer to His will.

I was learning, not perfectly but faithfully. I was not ignoring my emotions or pretending they were not real. I was finally surrendering them. I let myself feel them, but I no longer let them dictate my choices. For the first time, I stopped carrying what was never mine to carry.

Detachment, I came to see is not pretending you do not care. It is not shutting down or becoming numb. It is surrender. Not because it did not matter, but because it mattered so much that I had to place it in God's hands. To me, that was the truest kind of care. It was caring enough to trust it to the One greater than me. For me, detachment became a release that whispered, "I still feel it. I still remember. But I trust God with it now." That kind of letting go became the soil where healing could finally grow. I started breathing easier, laughing more, and living in the moment instead of replaying the past. Peace began to take root where anxiety had lived for years.

I used to live under what I call the law of limitations. I believed I was not enough, that love had to be earned, and that approval had to be chased just to feel worthy. But that was never God's law. That was the voice of fear and shame. It came out of wounds I had not yet faced. It kept me small, kept me searching. But the moment I let go of the fantasy, I realized I was already chosen. God had already called me worthy. He had already declared me enough. As His Word says in 1 Peter 2:9, I am part of a chosen people, a royal priesthood, God's special possession, called out of darkness into His wonderful light. That was the day the law of limitation finally lost its grip on me.

I did not see it all at once. Sometimes that law crept in quietly, disguised as something good. There were times I thought I was free, only to realize I was still measuring myself by the hope of being chosen. But slowly, patiently, God untangled those lies and replaced them with His truth.

In this new season, my focus shifted. It was no longer on who would affirm me. It was on what God was teaching me in surrender. For so long I thought becoming whole depended on someone else's role in my story. But as I prayed, processed, and walked with Him, I came to understand the truth. Wholeness was about the deeper work He was doing in my heart and the greater love He was forming in me.

That love was agape love, godly love. It was a love that prays, a love that intercedes, a love that protects without clinging, a love that is sacred. Even when emotions rose up strong, I had to learn not to let them lead me. I had to be honest about them but not let them carry me blindly.

My prayers are different now. I pray for clarity, strength, and peace. I pray for the woman I have finally embraced. And I thank God every single day for the wisdom and steadiness He gives me. This season did not just change me. It revealed me. It reminded me that becoming her is not one single moment but a daily choice. A choice to walk in truth and stay rooted in His presence.

I see her now in the smallest details: the way she guards her peace with confidence, the way she laughs without fear of tomorrow, the way she refuses to shrink herself for someone else's comfort. She is steady because her foundation is unshakable. She is whole because she no longer searches for worth outside of God. She is free because she has stopped trying to rewrite her past and instead carries it openly as testimony.

From here, the journey does not end. There are still prayers to pray, promises to hold on to, and callings to walk out with courage. I move forward with quiet confidence, knowing whatever comes next will meet me here, in this place of wholeness. Challenges will come, but they will not shake my identity. Seasons will shift, but they will not move me from my foundation. This is what becoming her looks like, not only in the beautiful moments, but also in the hidden days when faith is the only thing I have left to hold on to. In that quiet surrender, God began to open my eyes, revealing the depth of my assignment and the purpose He had placed in my life.

Becoming her was not the end of the journey. It was only the beginning to see God's hand move in ways I could not explain. As I embraced the woman, He was shaping me into, I noticed His presence grow louder and His Spirit confirm what I could not have known on my own. What I thought was healing was actually preparation. God was setting the stage for a deeper unveiling, a divine revelation that would shift how I saw Him, how I saw myself, and how I walked in my calling.

Chapter 9 Reflection

1. What does union with yourself and with God look like for you right now?

____

____

____

____

2. Have you ever mistaken deep spiritual love for romantic love? How did God help you see the difference?

____

____

____

____

3. What does sacred detachment mean to you, and how have you practiced it in your own journey?

____

____

____

____

4. In what ways has someone unknowingly awakened something in you that led you back to God?

____

____

____

____

5. How has your understanding of love, healing, and purpose deepened through your own fire moments?

____

____

____

____

Reflection Notes

Devine Revelation

Chapter 10 : **Divine Revelation**

As God worked on my vision, I started noticing something I had never paid much attention to before. It was shockingly easy to misread things when I was not filtering them through His Spirit. Back then, I would see numbers or patterns and call them confirmations from Him. Later, He showed me clearly: His presence was not hiding in the numbers or the signs. His presence was in my heart being lined up with His. That revelation was huge for me. It opened the door to something deeper, something real. I realized I had been trusting in practices that were never from Him to begin with.

For a while, I honestly thought manifestation was harmless. I told myself that if I just spoke it enough, I could make it happen. I even tried to speak outcomes into existence. I convinced myself it was only positive thinking. But God, in His mercy, opened my eyes wide.

He let me see that I was leaning on my own will and not on His.

At first, I did not even recognize the danger. Affirmations felt good. Focusing on my thoughts felt good, even spiritual. But that was the trap. They were distractions, pulling me away from the true source of peace and purpose. God had to keep showing me again and again that those practices were not from Him, no matter how nice they sounded.

The truth is that all those practices were empty. They could not heal my heart, give me peace, or draw me closer to Him. Through His Word, He reminded me that leaning on anything other than Him is dangerous. Jeremiah 17:5 says, "Cursed is the one who trusts in man, who draws strength from mere flesh, and whose heart turns away from the Lord." That verse hit me hard. It stopped me in my tracks. Even though I thought I was being innocent, I had been leaning on the wrong source the whole time.

Romans 12:2 also came alive to me: "Do not conform to the pattern of this world but be transformed by the renewing of your mind. Then you will be able to test and approve what God's will is, His good, pleasing and perfect will." When I read that, I saw it plain. The teachings I had been following were shaping me into the world's way of thinking. They were not renewing me in His Spirit. That revelation was not only a warning. It was an invitation. An invitation to real freedom, to clarity I had never known.

I began to see how easily deception can disguise itself as light. Some teachings sound spiritual, but they are not rooted in God. Ideas like vibrations, energy, and frequencies may sound harmless, but slowly they pull the heart away from Him. The Lord sharpened my discernment during that season. He reminded me His Spirit, His Word, and His voice were all I truly needed.

Real revelation does not come from numbers, signs, or secret codes. It comes from staying close to Him, listening to His Spirit, and letting His truth reshape my mind. Proverbs 3:5–6 says, "Trust in the Lord with all your heart and lean not on your own understanding; in all your ways submit to Him, and He will make your paths straight." My heart had to learn how to trust again. My mind had to let go of illusions I had been clinging to. My spirit had to come into alignment with the Creator, not with ideas that only looked promising on the outside.

That revelation changed me. It separated truth from lies. What I once thought was confusion turned into clarity. What I thought was harmless turned into lessons in discernment. And God, in His kindness, never shamed me for being naïve. He simply opened my eyes, and He did it gently.

That moment became a turning point. It was not the very beginning of my awakening, but it was the moment He revealed the danger of looking for guidance outside of

Him. He taught me to treasure His Word above every other voice. He showed me true connection with Him is not about what I can force into being. It is about surrender, about obedience, about letting His Spirit lead my life instead of me trying to lead myself.

I am grateful for that revelation. It reminded me that His ways are higher than mine. His truth cannot be shaken. His voice is the one I have to follow, no matter what. Every mistake, every lesson, even the times I thought manifestation was harmless, He used to prepare me for a life grounded in Him.

God showed me awakening does not come from techniques or formulas. It does not come from trying to control results. Awakening comes from trust. It comes from giving everything over to Him and letting His Word be the guide. I also began to see how the enemy uses distractions that look like light to pull people off course. But His Spirit kept revealing truth to me, and I could not ignore it. The questions and doubts I once carried were not failures. They were actually invitations to go deeper with Him.

The confusion I once stumbled through became God's preparation for something greater than I could have ever imagined.

Chapter 10 Reflection

1. Have you ever relied on your own words, thoughts, or practices instead of fully trusting God? What did you learn from that experience?

____

____

____

____

2. Romans 12:2 speak about renewing the mind. In what areas of your life do you feel God is asking you to renew your thoughts through His Word?

____

____

____

____

3. Are there practices, habits, or beliefs you once thought were harmless that God has since shown you were pulling you away from Him?

____

____

____

____

4. Proverbs 3:5–6 calls us to trust in the Lord rather than lean on our own understanding. What does that look like in your current season?

____

____

____

____

5. When has God given you a revelation that opened your eyes to truth you had not seen before? How did it change your walk with Him?

____

____

____

____

Reflection Notes

You're Not Crazy. You're Called.

Chapter 11: **You're Not Crazy. You're Called.**

There comes a moment on the journey, especially a spiritual one, when you start to question everything. You question your mind, your heart, your memories, and even your sanity. You begin to wonder if anyone will believe you. It feels like no one will believe you. You question whether you can trust your own judgment. The situation does not make sense. At times it seems impossible to understand. And sometimes, even in prayer, you feel like you are just making things up in your head. But in those moments, God reminds you: You are not crazy. You are called.

A calling rarely appears with perfect clarity. It often shows up disguised as confusion, heartbreak, or loss. Ask Moses. Ask Esther. Ask Mary. Ask Paul. Each of them was shaken before they were sent. Their minds were tested long before their missions became clear. Sometimes God has to tear down the comfortable and familiar to build you into who He created you to be. The enemy will try to convince you that the fire you are walking through is proof you have lost your mind. But perhaps it is proof you are finally waking up. Often what the world calls insanity is actually the beginning of an awakening through the Holy Spirit.

1 Corinthians 2:14 reminds us that the person without the Spirit cannot understand the things that come from the Spirit of God. Sometimes those most in tune with the Spirit are the very ones the world tries hardest to silence. If you are sensing things others do not understand, if God keeps confirming His Word to you in undeniable ways, if you are asking questions no one else is asking, you are not crazy. You are being called higher. It is not obsession. It is revelation. It is not delusion. It is divine preparation. God is refining you for something uncommon. You were not created to blend in. You were created to wake up to His truth.

Looking back at the dream I shared in Chapter 1, I see now it was never about a man at all. It was always about God calling me to my purpose. The longing in that moment was not about a relationship. It was a deeper, divine restoration. What started as confusion in that dream is now clear. I see it as God drawing me back to Him, using the dream to open my heart to His calling. The window in the dream felt like vision, as though God was letting me see what was ahead before I could fully step into it. The pole, I now believe, represented the Cross, the place where love had already been waiting and fulfillment had already been made available. Perhaps I could not reach God in the dream because I had not fully surrendered yet. Perhaps there were still parts of me that needed healing, layers He was gently peeling back.

Some things in life do not come with explanations, only feelings. Feelings that wake you in the night. A fire in your soul you cannot ignore. You do not always know where it is leading, but somehow you know it is God. That is how this journey began. Not with clarity, but with a calling I could not shake. I had built a peaceful life in another country, one where no one used the name tied to my purpose. I tried to hide, let go of ministry, titles, and dreams I did not ask for. But God does not forget what He placed in you. You can run, but eventually the call catches up.

In the past, the enemy would have tried to plant words like twin flame in my thoughts, a counterfeit idea meant to confuse what God was actually calling me to. And for a season, I entertained things that did not line up with God's Word, ideas that sounded spiritual but were not rooted in Him. I thought I was just being open minded, even enlightened. But little by little, God began to pull the veil back. He showed me that not everything labeled spiritual is from Him, and not every light comes from the true Light. When God opened my eyes, I could not unsee it. And once you see the truth, you can never go back to the lie.

During that season, I came across ideas like kundalini, angel numbers, vibrations, energies, and manifestation. I used to try to manifest during so-called spiritual gateways, believing certain times or seasons carried special power. But many of those manifestations never came to pass, and now I understand why. They were not God's will for my life. What I thought I could create on my own was never mine to claim. Only God decides the timing, the doors, and the blessings, and His will is always better than anything I could have tried to force. At first, I wondered if these ideas explained the stirring inside me, the fire that felt so personal and so real. For a moment, I thought they held the answers. I even tried to follow those signs, seeing repeating numbers on billboards, chasing patterns, convincing myself they were messages from God. It felt spiritual, but deep down I was still searching.

Then, in His mercy, the Lord revealed the truth. It was not mystical energy at all. It was His Spirit. That fire within me, that undeniable stirring, was the Holy Spirit awakening me, drawing me back, and beginning to guide me toward the path He had prepared. What I thought was revelation was actually distraction. Those so-called signs were pulling me away from the clarity and truth I was really seeking.

Now, when I see 2:31 on the clock, I no longer chase after it or try to decode its meaning. Instead, I pause and pray, Lord, bring structure, bring clarity, and touch the heart. What once drew me into confusion has now become a habit of intercession, a gentle reminder to look to God and not to signs.

Colossians 2:8 says, "See to it that no one takes you captive through hollow and deceptive philosophy, which depends on human tradition and the elemental spiritual forces of this world rather than on Christ." God revealed to me that affirmations on their own were never enough. They sounded positive, but they were not truly biblical. Positive affirmations rely on my words. Biblical declarations rely on God's Word, and only His Word brings real authority and transformation.

Instead of saying I am strong, I began to declare Philippians 4:13: I can do all things through Christ who strengthens me. Instead of repeating that I had money, I began to stand on Philippians 4:19: But my God shall supply all your need according to his riches in glory by Christ Jesus. My words had no power on their own, but His Word carries eternal power and authority.

This is why I share my story. Because my journey was never about chasing New Age practices. It was always about finding my way back to God. It was only later, in His divine revelation, that He opened my eyes to the counterfeits I had brushed against. And once God revealed the truth, I could never unsee it.

Looking back, I see now that all of this was training ground. Even in my lowest, God used moments of obedience to wake me up. From start to finish, it was always Him. He was calling me back to prayer, back to fire, and back to truth.

You are not crazy. You are called. The very thing you thought would destroy you was the tool God used to deliver you into purpose.

God never wastes anything. He will take the tears, the silence, the questions, and even the mistakes, and turn them into preparation. That is what He did for me. And if He did it for me, He can do it for you.

To the one still wondering if the pain was for nothing, hear this: not a single tear, not a single night of questioning was overlooked. God has been weaving every moment into His plan for you. Your scars are not the end of your story. They are the beginning of your assignment. The wilderness was training, the silence was preparation, and the fire was purification. And now, the same God who carried you through it will use it to carry others.

This is the truth you cannot escape. What was meant to destroy you has positioned you for destiny. You are not forgotten. You are not disqualified. You are chosen. And one day, you will see clearly what I came to see. Your pain always carried purpose, because God was writing glory into your story from the very beginning.

The fire was never meant to consume you. It was meant to refine you. Every flame you walked through, every ache you carried, every question that kept you awake, was drawing you closer to the One your soul had always known. Do not despise the fire you had to walk through, because it is the fire that prepared you.

Do not curse the breaking, because it was the breaking that made you whole. And when you rise, and you will rise, the world will see that the hand of God was on you the entire time.

Chapter 11 Reflection

1. Have you ever questioned your calling because of how unusual or intense your journey has felt? What reminded you that you weren't crazy, you were called?

____

____

____

____

2. How do you relate to Sharon's shift from chasing clarity to trusting in God's preparation?

____

____

____

____

3. What does the dream she described reveal to you about how God might be using symbols and visions in your life?

____

____

____

____

4. How has God used fire, whether emotional, spiritual, or circumstantial, to refine your purpose or identity?

____

____

____

____

5. What sacred truth about yourself or your walk with God are you beginning to remember more clearly now?

____

____

____

____

Reflection Notes

A Prophetic Prayer for the Reader

Lord, I thank You for the one holding this book right now. You see them. You know what they carry. You know the questions they've asked when no one else was around and the ache they can't always put into words. Be near to them now and let them know they are not alone.

In Jesus' name I speak to the places in them that have been aching, come alive. What felt like longing, let it be met with Your presence. What felt like loss, let it open the way for Your glory. I declare this with boldness: your pain has purpose. Every tear, every heartbreak, every hidden place of suffering has been seen by God.

You are the Redeemer. You take what was meant for harm and turn it into fire that shapes and refines. Beauty out of ashes. Strength out of weakness. I pray against every false voice and every false light that tried to pull them away from You. Lies are broken, confusion is lifted, and truth takes its place. Let their heart be aligned with You and let restoration come.

I break the lie that said they weren't enough. That lie is silenced now. You are seen. You are known. You are deeply loved by the One who created you. And I declare this: the fire on your life will not destroy you. It will refine you; it will mark you, and it will set you apart. Now step into your purpose and into the future God has written for you.

In Jesus' name, Amen.

About the Author

My name is Sharon Washington, and life has taken me through many different seasons. For six years I lived and taught in the Middle East. My classroom wasn't just about reading lessons or math problems. It was a place where students found encouragement, where they knew someone believed in them. Those years changed me too, teaching me patience, resilience, and the beauty of seeing the world through many different cultures.

Now I live in Texas, walking through a season of healing and restoration. I am a mother and a grandmother, and my family is one of my greatest joys. They remind me daily that God has been faithful through every twist and turn of my story.

Writing this book has been part of that journey. It gave me a way to put my experiences into words and share them honestly. My hope is that others who pick up these pages will see a piece of their own story and realize they are not alone.

If this book has touched your life, I would love to hear from you. You can reach me at roseofsharonministry2.1@gmail.com.

Made in the USA
Coppell, TX
30 December 2025

67833084R00083